WHAT IF...

AIRPLANES

Steve Parker

Copper Beech Books
Brookfield, Connecticut

CONTENTS

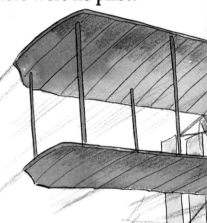

© Aladdin Books Ltd 1995

Designed and produced by
Aladdin Books Ltd
28 Percy Street
London W1P 0LD

Editor
Jon Richards

First published in the United States
in 1995 by
Copper Beech Books
an imprint of Millbrook Press
2 Old New Milford Road
Brookfield, Connecticut 06804

Designed by
David West Children's Book Design
Designers
Rob Shone, Flick Killerby,
Edward Simkins
Illustrator
Peter Wilks – Simon Girling and
Associates

Printed in Belgium

Library of Congress Cataloging-in-
Publication Data

Parker, Steve.
Airplanes / by Steve Parker ;
illustrated by Peter Wilks. p. cm. --
(What if...) Includes index.
Summary: An imaginative look at
airplanes through such questions as
"What if airplanes didn't have air?"
and "What if airplanes could go into
space?"
ISBN 1-56294-911-X (lib. bdg.) --
ISBN 1-56294-946-2 (pbk.)
1. Airplanes--Juvenile literature. [1.
Airplanes--Miscellanea. 2. Questions
and Answers.] I. Wilks, Peter. ill. II.
Title. III. Series: Parker, Steve. What
if.--TL547.P268 1995 95-23981--
629.13--dc20 CIP AC

WHAT IF THERE WERE NO INTRODUCTION?

Well, you wouldn't be reading this! The *What If...?* books look at things from a very unusual angle, to make them exciting and interesting, as well as being packed with facts and fun.

Have you ever traveled in a flying machine? It might be a balloon, airship, glider, small plane, or even a jetliner. If so, you know what an amazing experience it is. All kinds of aircraft soar through the skies. They carry people and cargo, take tourists on exotic vacations to faraway places, transport politicians and business people to world summits, dash to emergencies and rescues, spy on others, patrol against enemy invasion – and even look out for aliens in their UFOs!

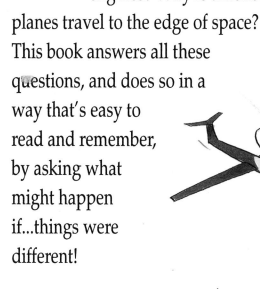

What If Airplanes...? peeks into, around, and behind these various aircraft, to see how, and why they work. You can find out about the pioneers of flying, how the jet engine makes its screaming whine, why flying boats were once popular, and what would happen if planes had their wings on upside down. How do pilots fly in the dark? Why do some planes lack engines? Why is a helicopter called a rotary-winged aircraft, and which planes travel to the edge of space? This book answers all these questions, and does so in a way that's easy to read and remember, by asking what might happen if...things were different!

WHAT IF AIRCRAFT DIDN'T HAVE WINGS?

Most of them would speed along the runway... and crash at the end, without taking off. Wings make a plane rise into the air, by providing lift. The wing shape also tells you how fast a plane goes. Slower planes, especially gliders, have very long, thin wings that stick out sideways. These wings have a very narrow chord (the distance from the front of the wing – leading edge – to the rear of the wing – trailing edge). This is the same design as the wings of gliding birds, like the albatross. Faster planes have swept-back wings, usually with a bigger chord, like fast hunting birds such as hawks.

An uplifting experience

Some aircraft don't get their lift from wings. It comes from a jet engine or propeller facing straight down, which pushes the aircraft into the air. A strange test craft from the 1950s, called the "Flying Bedstead," did this. So does the Harrier Jump Jet, which can take off straight up, and hover in mid-air. Hovercraft use lifting fans, like propellers facing downward, to create a cushion of air.

What if a plane flew upside down?

First, how does a wing work? Seen end-on, a wing has a special shape, known as the airfoil section. It is more curved on top than below. As the plane flies, air going over the wing has farther to travel than air beneath. This means the air over the top moves faster, which produces low pressure, so the wing is pushed upward – a force known as *lift* – which raises the plane. If a plane flew upside down, the wing would not give any lift. To overcome this, the plane tilts its nose up at a steep angle. Air hitting the wing then pushes it up, keeping the plane in the air.

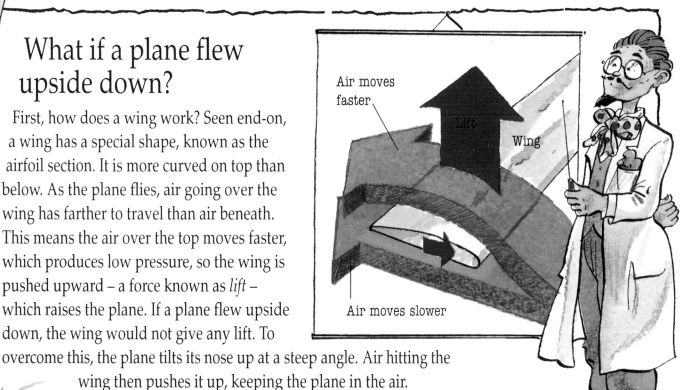

Air moves faster

Lift

Wing

Air moves slower

Can planes fly in space?

A few can, like the X-15 rocket planes of the 1960s and the space shuttles of today. First, they need engine power to blast up there. The X-15 was carried up on a converted B-52 bomber, while today the shuttle uses massive rocket boosters. Once in space, there's no air (or anything else), so wings can't work by providing lift. The power for all maneuvers in space comes from small rocket thrusters.

How do spy planes fly so high?

Spy planes, such as the U-2 and the Blackbird, need to fly high, at 100,000 ft (30,000 m) or higher, so they are beyond detection by enemy planes or radar. However, as air is very thin at such heights, they need very special wing designs, with an extra-curved top surface, to give the greatest possible lift. With the arrival of spy satellites, the use of spy planes declined, until recently. A new generation of pilotless, remote-control spy planes, such as DarkStar, has arrived.

WHAT IF ANIMALS DIDN'T HAVE WINGS?

They couldn't fly, either. Only three groups of animals can fly with complete control. These are insects, birds, and bats. Many other "flying" creatures, such as flying squirrels, are really only gliders, just able to swoop down to the ground. The true fliers beat their wings up and down, to give both lift and forward thrust. Their bodies have many special features. They are lightweight, yet have strong muscles to move their wings. If humans had wings, our chest and shoulder muscles would need to be huge to flap them, and our legs would be tiny to save weight!

Vertical muscles contract, wings flip up

Horizontal muscles contract, wings flop down

Flying insects

In an insect, like a bee, the middle part of the body, or thorax, contains two sets of muscles. The wings are fixed to the outer case of the thorax. As the muscles contract they pull the wings up and down.

Membrane

Going batty!

Bats fly by flapping their arms, which have become long, large wings during millions of years of evolution. A bat's finger bones are extremely long. They support the wing membrane, which is incredibly thin, yet stretchy and strong. The fingers can make the wing twist to change direction, and fold it away after use as an upside-down sleeping bag!

Fingers

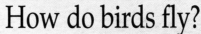

Pectoral muscles

Downstroke

Upstroke

How do birds fly?

They go flap-flap-flap! As in bats, the bird's arms have evolved into wings. Very strong muscles in the chest pull the wings down. This pushes air down, and pushes the bird up. The wings and feathers are angled so that some air is pushed backward too, giving the bird forward movement. Smaller muscles pull the wings up. During this upstroke the feathers twist so that air can pass through them, otherwise the bird would just push itself down again!

Thin walls

Cross-struts

What if a bird wanted to save weight?

Natural evolution has already produced lots of weight-saving features. These include thin-walled bones with air spaces for lightness and cross-struts for strength. Feathers also weigh hardly anything, yet they give a bird a streamlined body, a warm coat, and colors for camouflage.

A load of hot air

Birds can stay up for hours by using rising currents of warm air, called thermals. The bird circles around these to rise up, before gliding to another thermal. Glider pilots also use thermals to stay aloft.

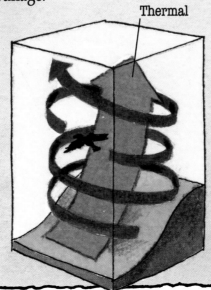

Thermal

Human-powered flight

Human legs are strong enough to get the body airborne, with a little help from machinery. The Gossamer Albatross crossed the English Channel between France and England in 1979, using only a human cyclist to keep it in the air.

WHAT IF PLANES DIDN'T HAVE TAILS?

They would be impossible to steer or control! The tail has important parts called stabilizers and control surfaces. The upright stabilizer, or fin, stops the plane from swinging side to side. Attached to the back of the fin is the rudder, for steering left to right. The small, rear stabilizers, or tailplane stop the plane from wobbling up and down. Hinged to their rear are the elevators, for climbing or diving.

Aileron
Controls roll, which is the plane leaning or tilting to the side, for turning, or even spinning right over in a corkscrew-like path.

Rudder
Controls yaw, which is the plane turning left or right.

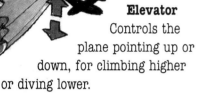

Are there planes without tails?

Yes, a few. Stealth planes are designed to be invisible on radar, so they lack an upright stabilizer (fin) because this shows up well on radar.

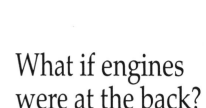

Elevator
Controls the plane pointing up or down, for climbing higher or diving lower.

What if engines were at the back?

Some are! However, you would have to move the tailplane and fin somewhere else. The fin's task might be done by vertilizers (vertical stabilizers) at the ends of the wings. The tailplane's job could be done by small foreplane wings at the front, called *canards*.

How many wings does a plane need?

In the early days, when wing design was just beginning, and engines were not very powerful, many planes, called biplanes, had two sets of wings. The Phillips Multiplane of 1907 had 21 small, thin wings! But it crashed into pieces.

What if planes were like paper darts?

One almost is. Concorde has long, triangular wings along the sides of the fuselage (body), called *delta wings*. These give good lift and stability at high speeds, since Concorde cruises at more than Mach 2 (twice the speed of sound) – 1,320 mph (2,125 km/h).

Swinging wings

Some planes have swing-wings. They are called "variable geometry" combat jets, and they take off and land on a very short runway, such as the deck of an aircraft carrier. The wings swing sideways for take off, slow flight and landing, and then swing back for superfast speed.

WHAT IF PLANES COULD LAND ON WATER?

Many can. In an emergency, the pilot can "ditch" the plane onto water. It's very risky and the plane usually sinks – but at least the crew and passengers have a chance of survival. Seaplanes are different. They are designed to take off and land on water. Instead of wheels, they have long, streamlined floats that slip smoothly over the surface. The flying boat is a type of seaplane with a boat-shaped fuselage (body) that rests in the water. Flying boats were popular when air travel began in the 1930s. Few big cities had airports with long runways, but many were near water. Today, seaplanes are useful in places that have many islands and few landing strips.

Can seaplanes land on land?

Some can. They have wheels that stick out slightly below the floats, so they can touch down on water or land. They are called *amphibious aircraft*. One problem is that floats are quite large, so they make the plane fly slower and use more fuel, compared to wheels which can be retracted.

Skimming above the waves

One of the latest developments for seaplanes is the *ground effect* plane. Developed by Russia, the ground effect plane traps air underneath its wings to create a cushion, on which the plane skims over the waves. A hovercraft uses the same principle.

Which boat has wings?

The hydrofoil is a boat that has ski-like wings on stilts under its hull. As it picks up speed, the wings provide lift in the water (like a plane's wings in the air). This makes the hull rise out of the water. The hydrofoil can then travel at great speed because less of the boat is in contact with the water, skimming across the surface.

How big are seaplanes?

The flying boat Hughes H4 Hercules, nicknamed the Spruce Goose, has the longest wingspan of any airplane, at 327 ft (98 m) – as big as a soccer field. A Boeing 747 Jumbo Jet's wings are 200 ft (60 m) long. The H4 was built in 1947 and flew only once, just 3,000 ft (1,000 m).

Can aircraft land on ships?

Yes. Helicopters can land on a small platform which can be fitted to any reasonably sized ship. Navy ships called aircraft carriers have a long, wide, flat deck for takeoffs and landings by special carrier-borne planes. These shipboard jet fighters include the Sea Harrier Jump Jet, the F-14 Tomcat, and the F-18 Hornet.

WHAT IF THE WRIGHT BROTHERS HAD STUCK TO CYCLING?

Yes, it's true. Wilbur and Orville Wright were really bicycle mechanics! In the late 19th century, the new craze was the "safety cycle." In their hometown of Dayton, Ohio, the Wright brothers set up a business manufacturing and selling bicycles. In 1903, they attached an engine to a glider and produced the *Flyer*. Orville piloted the Flyer on the world's first airplane flight December 17, 1903 at Kitty Hawk, North Carolina.

What if Louis Blériot had taken off late?

He might not have been first to fly the English Channel, on July 25, 1909. He had to fly between dawn and dusk, so the aviator took off from Calais at 4:40 a.m. After traveling 23 miles (37 km), he landed in Dover, England.

On the rocks!

Between June 14 and 15, 1919, British airmen John Alcock and Arthur Brown made the first non-stop flight across the Atlantic Ocean. They flew from Newfoundland, Canada, to Ireland, in a converted Vickers Vimy. In a snowstorm, a fuel gauge became iced over. So Brown climbed out to knock the ice away. A build up of ice could have caused the plane to crash!

How did Charles Lindbergh stay awake?

He had to – he was first to fly solo non-stop across the Atlantic, from New York to Paris, on May 20 to 21, 1927. The trip, in his Ryan Monoplane *Spirit of St. Louis*, was 3,631 miles (5,810 km) and took 33 hours 29 minutes. A former airmail pilot, Lindbergh dozed off several times. He woke as the plane went out of control, diving and spinning toward the waves. But he quickly became alert when he reached Ireland's rocky coast, and flew on to a huge crowd in France.

Do planes get faster and faster?

They certainly do! Since the first powered flight by the Wright brothers, people have tried to fly faster and faster. The Wright Flyer managed about 31 mph (50 km/h) in its short flight at Kitty Hawk. By the 1930s, planes, such as the GB Sportster (above) were zooming through the sky at 296 mph (477 km/h). Since then, the advent of the jet and rocket age has pushed airplanes faster. The fastest airspeed was achieved in a Lockheed SR-71A "Blackbird," flying at 2,193 mph (3,530 km/h) in 1976.

WHAT IF A HELICOPTER HAD NO REAR PROPELLER?

The main "propeller" on top of a helicopter is the main rotor, and the small propeller at the rear is the tail rotor. Without a tail rotor, as the main rotor spun around one way, the helicopter would spin the other! This is due to a basic law of science – Newton's third law of motion, which says that every action has an equal and opposite reaction. So the pilot and passengers would get very dizzy and the helicopter would be impossible to control!

How are the rotor blades controlled?

By a complicated device in the middle of the rotors, called the *rotor head*. It has a double ring, called the swashplate. The lower ring is moved up and down and tilted by the pilot's control levers and pedals, and the upper one spins with the rotors. By a complicated system of hinges, levers, and bearings, the swashplate makes the rotors change their height and pitch (slope or angle), to give more lift for climbing, or less lift for descending.

Main drive shaft

Swashplate upper ring

Swashplate lower ring

What if a helicopter had two main rotors?

Their blades might crash into each other! If the rotors were at slightly different heights, and linked by gears, their blades could always move between each other. This happens on twin-rotor helicopters like the CH-47 Chinook. The rotors go in opposite directions, so there's no need for a tail rotor.

What if a rotor had no engine?

Can a plane fly like a helicopter?

The Bell-Boeing V-22 Osprey can. Its engines and propellers can tilt, so that the Osprey can take off or land vertically and even hover, like a helicopter. The engine then slowly tilts forward so that the Osprey can fly normally.

An autogyro has a normal engine and propeller, and a large helicopter-like rotor that is unpowered. The forward movement makes the rotor swirl around and provide lift, so this craft doesn't need wings.

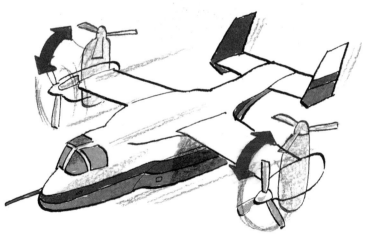

Is it difficult to fly a helicopter?

For most people, yes. The helicopter is an unstable design, and without the pilot's constant attention, it would spin out of control. Foot pedals control the tail rotor. The cyclic pitch control lever in front tilts the rotors to fly forward, backward, or sideways. The collective pitch control lever at the side alters the rotors to climb or descend. Its engine throttle twist-grip changes engine speed. That's five controls at once!

Cyclic pitch control lever   Collective pitch control lever

Rudder pedals

WHAT IF A PLANE HAD NO ENGINE?

Most planes can glide down in an emergency, like when the engine is falling out. But a plane that's designed to have no engine is a glider, or perhaps a hang glider. These unpowered aircraft sail and soar silently through the air. They always glide downward against the air around them, but they do so very gradually, because of their light weight and excellent aerodynamic shapes. The best gliders travel over 196 ft (60 m) yet descend only 3ft (1 m). The key to gliding is to find air that's moving upward faster than your glider is going downward, such as a thermal (see page 7). A cockpit instrument called the *compensated variometer* shows how fast the air outside is moving up or down, no matter what the vertical speed or maneuvers of the glider itself. Once in this rising air, the glider will circle, and gain height.

How do gliders take off?

In the past, gliders have been launched off cliffs, and catapulted by bungee cords. Some were even towed behind cars. One method used today is the fast-running winch that winds in the tow-rope attached to the glider. Most popular is aero-towing behind a small plane.

Do some pilots hang around all day?

In a hang glider, the pilot hangs below a large V-shaped wing made of flexible material stretched over a metal-tube frame. The pilot steers by shifting his or her body weight to make the aircraft move up, down, or sideways. The world-record distance for a real glider is 913 miles (1,460 km), and for a hang glider, 305 miles (488 km).

Which glider fits in a backpack?

The modern parachute has several sections called *cells* and works partly like a glider. It can be controlled and steered by pulling on cords. Using one of these parachutes, and helped by thermals, a parachutist can stay in the air for 40 minutes.

What if your parachute didn't open?

This hardly ever happens. Parachutes are thoroughly checked and packed very carefully into their bags, so that they open properly every time. However, there is a reserve parachute for use in emergencies, because it is smaller.

Getting heavy!

Big military gliders can carry troops and several tons of equipment, such as large guns and even jeeps. A jumbo-sized glider could even carry jumbo-sized cargo such as elephants! The world's biggest glider is the space shuttle, which comes down to land at 219 mph (350 km/h).

WHAT IF AIRCRAFT PROPELLERS PUSHED AND PULLED?

They do, depending on which way they spin. So it's important to make the engine work only one way, or the plane might shoot backward! A propeller (prop) at the front pulls the plane, while the one at the back pushes it. Both work in the same way, as shown below.

Can propellers work at the back?

Back propellers are known as *pusherprops*. They spin and work in the same way as *pullerprops* (front propellers). They're used in modern microlights and slow-flying survey aircraft. With a pusher-prop, the pilot has a good view and does not get wind and noise from the blades. But aerial control is better with pullerprops.

How do propellers work?

Air pushed backward

Forward thrust

First, each blade has an airfoil section, like a mini-wing. It creates low air pressure in front and higher air pressure behind. This pulls the plane forward.

Secondly, a propeller's long blades are angled. As they rotate, they push air backward and pull themselves forward.

How many blades can a prop have?

The number depends on features such as the size and power of the engine turning it, the design of the whole plane, and how fast you want to go. Many planes have two-bladed props. Multi-bladed props are heavier and need more powerful engines.

What if a propeller was attached to a jet?

It is, sort of. A turbofan is a jet engine with a huge, multi-bladed fan turbine at the front. This blows air at high pressure into the engine, as in a normal jet. It also blows air around the engine, like a prop (see page 20).

Fan turbine

Combustion chamber

How big can propellers be?

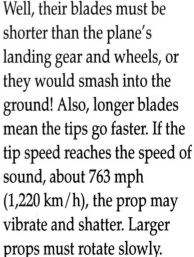

Why didn't war pilots shoot off their propellers?

In World War I (1914–1918), fighter planes had just been invented. At first, pilots shot with hand-held pistols or rifles. A machine gun in front of the pilot, where he could see to take aim, would be a good idea – but the bullets might hit the propeller! So in 1915, the designers of the German Fokker fighters invented a levers-and-gears device called the *interrupter*. It made sure the bullets fired between the blades as they whizzed around.

Well, their blades must be shorter than the plane's landing gear and wheels, or they would smash into the ground! Also, longer blades mean the tips go faster. If the tip speed reaches the speed of sound, about 763 mph (1,220 km/h), the prop may vibrate and shatter. Larger props must rotate slowly.

WHAT IF THE JET ENGINE HAD NEVER BEEN INVENTED?

Air travel and air battle would be much slower. The fastest jetliners, and the fastest military fighter and bomber aircraft, are all powered by jet engines. Only jets can move the average airliner along at 563 to 593 mph (900 to 950 km/h), which is nearly the speed of sound. An airliner with the other main type of propulsion, piston (internal combustion) engines turning propellers, could never keep up – no matter how many engines it had! And only jets can accelerate some fighters to more than 1,625 mph (2,600 km/h), like the McDonnell Douglas F-15 Eagle and the Russian MiG-25 Foxbat.

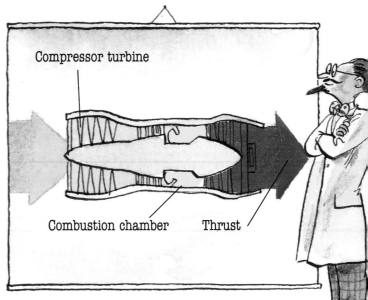

Compressor turbine

Combustion chamber   Thrust

How does a jet engine work?

It uses spinning angled blades called *turbines*, which work like powerful, high-speed fans. The jet engine sucks in air at the front, squeezes and squashes it with the compressor turbines, sprays fuel into it, and burns it in the combustion chamber as a continuous roaring explosion. The hot gases blast out of the back, and thrust the jet engine forward. As the gases leave, they spin the exhaust turbines, which are linked to, and drive, the compressor turbines. Other jets include the ramjet and turbofan (see page 19).

What if the whole engine spun around?

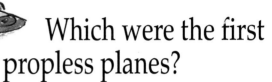

On some planes, it does! It's called a rotary engine and works basically like a car engine, with pistons going up and down inside cylinders. But a rotary engine has its cylinders in a circle, and they spin around and around.

Which were the first propless planes?

The first jet engines were revved up by English engineer Frank Whittle in 1937, but they were firmly fixed to his test bench. The first jet-powered airplane to fly was the German Heinkel He 178 in 1939, with an engine designed by Hans Pabst von Ohain. It was followed by the British Gloster Whittle, in 1941. The first jet aircraft to enter service was the British Gloster Meteor fighter, but the first to get into a fight was the Messerschmitt Me 262, in September 1944.

Silent night

Modern designs of turbofans are much quieter than the earlier turbojets. But many other things affect aircraft noise, such as the height of the plane. If an aircraft can take off very quickly and climb rapidly – Short Take-Off and Landing (STOL) – it soon seems quieter to people on the ground. Many city airports have rules governing noise limits and allow only STOL aircraft.

Could aircraft break the sound barrier?

Without jets, probably not. The fastest propeller-driven aircraft ever flown is the Russian TU-95/142, nicknamed the "Bear." It has been recorded flying at 575 mph (925 km/h) – that's four fifths the speed of sound. Almost, but not quite.

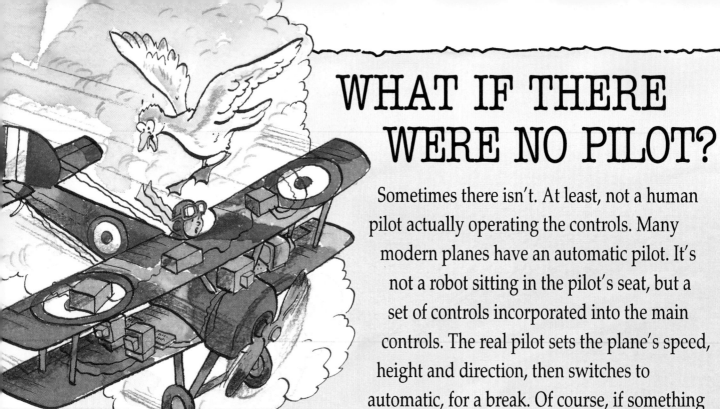

WHAT IF THERE WERE NO PILOT?

Sometimes there isn't. At least, not a human pilot actually operating the controls. Many modern planes have an automatic pilot. It's not a robot sitting in the pilot's seat, but a set of controls incorporated into the main controls. The real pilot sets the plane's speed, height and direction, then switches to automatic, for a break. Of course, if something happens, alarms activate, and the real pilot takes the controls. In very modern planes, the computer-based auto-pilot can even take off and land the aircraft.

How do pilots "fly by wire?"

Computer screens are wired up to show speed, direction, engine conditions, and other information. Small levers and switches activate the flaps, rudder, and other control surfaces. This happens by sending electrical signals along wires to motors. This system is all controlled by the avionics system.

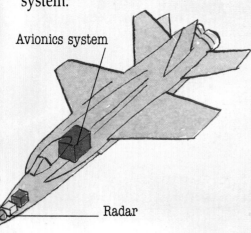

Avionics system

Radar

Tires, skis, skids, and floats

Airplanes can be equipped with a variety of landing gear, depending on their size and the conditions. Jet liners require wheels to withstand the pressure. Seaplanes need floats to keep them above water. Gliders and early rocket planes use skids, while planes that have to land on snow and ice use skis!

What is a "black box?"

It's not usually black or box-shaped. It may be bright orange and cylindrical. But it's the usual name for an aircraft's flight data recorder. This device continually records the plane's speed, height, direction, and other information from the instruments, as well as radio signals and voice communications. It is specially made to be fireproof, shockproof, and waterproof. In the event of emergency or disaster, it can be recovered, and its recordings give valuable information about what happened.

Do you have to be strong to fly a plane?

Not really. Some controls are simple electrical switches and knobs. Others are levers, like the control column and rudder pedals, but they are well-balanced with counterweights and cables, so they aren't too heavy to move. But to fly a plane well, you do have to be alert and physically fit, with good coordination and quick reactions.

When can you see two sets of controls and instruments?

In the "head-up display." There are not really two sets. Part of the main display is reflected or projected upward onto the front windshield or canopy, or into the pilot's special helmet visor. The pilot can look ahead and see outside, and the controls at the same time.

WHAT IF THE PILOT GOT LOST?

Can pilots see in the dark?

They can "see" using radar (RAdio Detection And Ranging). This works like a bat's hearing. It blips out radio signals, and detects the echoes that bounce off other planes or features, and then displays them on a screen. Radar was first used in World War II (1939 – 1945). To keep it secret, there was a rumor that the pilots ate lots of carrots to see in the dark!

A lost pilot could mean big trouble. He or she couldn't stop and ask someone the way. An airplane has a limited amount of fuel, and, sooner or later, it must land. What if the pilot is lost flying over mountains at this time, or thick woodland? What if it becomes foggy, or dark, and the pilot can't find the runway? This is why all pilots must learn about navigation: knowing where you are and where you're going. It can be done by many methods, such as using a compass and radar signals from ground beacons. The pilot can also talk to an air-traffic controller, and use modern satellite navigation, as well as looking out of the window!

Highways in the sky

The skies near busy airports get crowded, so there are flight corridors for planes going in certain directions. Each plane must know where to fly, and the speed and height it must travel – its flight path. The whole system is organized by air-traffic controllers who speak to all planes by radio, and by positional satellites. They make sure that there are no near misses (or should that be near hits?)

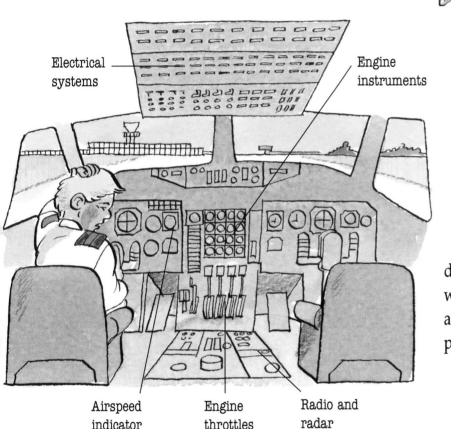

Electrical systems

Engine instruments

Airspeed indicator

Engine throttles

Radio and radar

How do pilots tell time?

In a modern jetliner, the time is one of several pieces of important information displayed by the instruments on the flight deck. These include air speed, altitude (height), a compass to show direction, and a radio to stay in touch with the ground control. The displays are on computer screens. A small plane simply has an ordinary clock!

How do pilots talk to people?

Not by shouting loudly! They talk over the plane's radio, mainly to air-traffic controllers in their control towers on the ground, and perhaps to the pilots of other planes, or meteorologists at weather stations. They might also chat to people from the airline about flight times or special passengers, or to the plane manufacturers if the aircraft is behaving strangely. The radio plays a vital role in keeping the pilot informed about what is happening outside the plane.

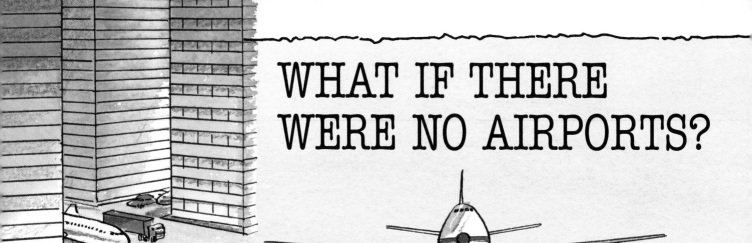

WHAT IF THERE WERE NO AIRPORTS?

Are there airports in cities?

Not in the very center. A plane taking off couldn't stop at red lights! But there are small airports very close to the city centers. They are used mainly by helicopters, small business jets, and STOL commuter planes (see page 21). Big airliners need very long runways and make too much noise, so their airports are usually several miles away from city centers. There are usually urban highways and public transportation to the city airports.

Landing a huge jetliner in a field would be impossible. It might hit a molehill or sink in the mud. Even if it landed, the passengers would not be pleased to find themselves in the middle of nowhere! Many modern planes need a straight, flat, hard-surfaced runway at least 9,842 ft (3,000 m) long, for safe takeoff and landing. In fact, most airports have two or more runways, facing different directions. This is because it's best for planes to take off or land into the wind. The air blowing at the plane and over the wings creates increased lift for the same speed relative to the ground. This gives quicker lift off and better control on touchdown.

Why can't you stack planes on top of each other?

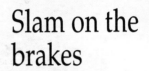

You can, if you are an air-traffic controller (see page 24). As planes wait to land at a busy airport, they fly in wide circles at certain heights, each several hundred feet above the next. When the runway is clear, the lowest one takes its final approach path and comes in to land. The others move down the stack level, one by one, from the lowest upward.

What if there were no air-traffic control?

At a busy international airport there is a takeoff or landing every 30 seconds. The air-traffic controllers speak by radio to the pilots, telling them which approach paths to follow, where to stack, and which runway to use for takeoff and landing. Otherwise, CRASH! BANG ! SMASH! CRUNCH!

Slam on the brakes

Many planes have brakes on their wheels to stop. Jets may have panels that fold out to deflect their exhaust gases forward. Other planes may use parachutes, or if they are to land on an aircraft carrier, a trailing hook that catches on wires on the deck.

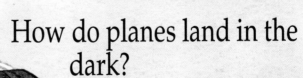

How do planes land in the dark?

The pilot does not use a torch or eat lots of carrots (see page 24). There are landing lights and radio beacons near the airport showing the direction and distance of the runway, and patterns of colored runway lights illuminating the landing area. Many planes have an Instrument Landing System (ILS). It detects radio signals sent from the airport to show if the pilot is landing safely.

WHAT IF THERE WERE NO PLANES?

Life would certainly be different. Airplanes play many vital roles throughout the world, carrying people and cargo to faraway places in only a fraction of the time it takes other forms of transportation. The sky might be full of balloons, slowly weaving about the sky. Instead of crossing the Atlantic in a couple of hours, it would take several days on an ocean liner, or stuck in a small basket under a balloon.

Can saucers fly?

They certainly can. Have you ever thrown a Frisbee and wondered why it can fly? That's because the shape of a Frisbee is similar to a plane's wing. It has an airfoil section which creates a higher pressure below its body than above as it passes through the air, producing lift. It achieves all this without the help of wings. Many planes can achieve the same effect by having their fuselage (body) shaped with an airfoil cross-section. They are known as *lifting bodies* and can fly with only very small wings.

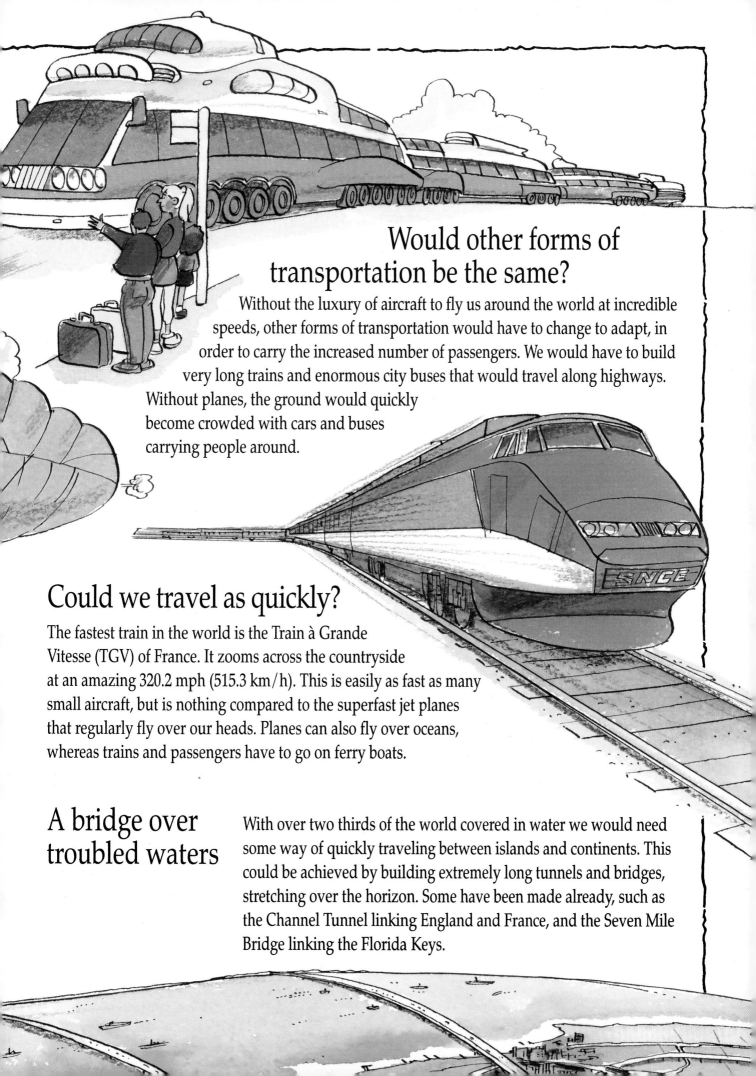

Would other forms of transportation be the same?

Without the luxury of aircraft to fly us around the world at incredible speeds, other forms of transportation would have to change to adapt, in order to carry the increased number of passengers. We would have to build very long trains and enormous city buses that would travel along highways. Without planes, the ground would quickly become crowded with cars and buses carrying people around.

Could we travel as quickly?

The fastest train in the world is the Train à Grande Vitesse (TGV) of France. It zooms across the countryside at an amazing 320.2 mph (515.3 km/h). This is easily as fast as many small aircraft, but is nothing compared to the superfast jet planes that regularly fly over our heads. Planes can also fly over oceans, whereas trains and passengers have to go on ferry boats.

A bridge over troubled waters

With over two thirds of the world covered in water we would need some way of quickly traveling between islands and continents. This could be achieved by building extremely long tunnels and bridges, stretching over the horizon. Some have been made already, such as the Channel Tunnel linking England and France, and the Seven Mile Bridge linking the Florida Keys.

GLOSSARY

airfoil section
The special shape of an aircraft wing or propeller when seen edge-on, with the upper surface more curved than the lower surface. This gives a difference in air pressure and creates the force called *lift*.

control surface
A panel on an aircraft that moves into the air flowing past, and helps to control the flight, such as the rudder.

fin
The "tail," the upright part or vertical stabilizer, which usually sticks up at the rear of a plane. The rudder is attached to the rear of the fin.

flight deck
The small room at the front of a large plane where the pilot and flight crew sit to control and fly the aircraft. On a small plane this is usually the *cockpit*.

fuselage
The main "body" of a plane, which is usually a long, thin tube carrying the pilot and crew, passengers, and freight.

Mach
A speed scale related to the speed of sound. Mach 1 is the speed of sound under given conditions such as pressure and temperature. Named after the Austrian scientist Ernst Mach (1838–1916).

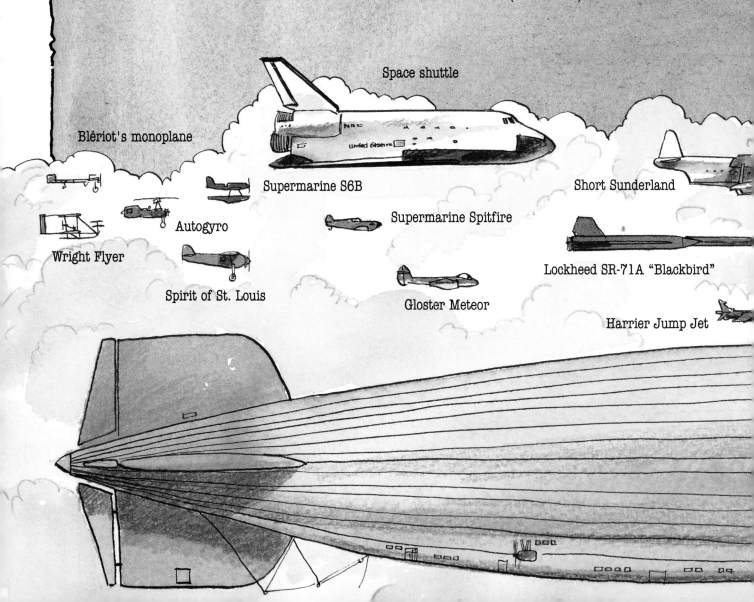

Space shuttle

Blériot's monoplane

Supermarine S6B

Short Sunderland

Autogyro

Supermarine Spitfire

Wright Flyer

Lockheed SR-71A "Blackbird"

Spirit of St. Louis

Gloster Meteor

Harrier Jump Jet

pitch
The angle of a plane when seen from the side – that is, whether it is pointing up or down, which usually means it will climb or dive.

roll
The angle of a plane when seen from the front (or back) – that is, whether it is leaning or tilted to one side, which usually means it will twist over in a corkscrew-like path.

rotors
The long propeller-like blades on top of a helicopter, which provide lift and also allow the helicopter to fly forward, backward, and sideways.

STOL
Short Take-Off and Landing, meaning an aircraft that can go up or come down on a short runway. This can be a couple of hundred feet long.

tailplane
The smaller wings or horizontal stabilizers sticking out sideways from the rear of a plane. The elevators are attached to the rear of it.

turbine
Set of fan-like angled blades used in many machines, such as power plant generators and aircraft engines.

variable geometry
The proper name for a "swing-wing" plane, where the main wings usually swing straight out sideways for slow flight, or take off and sweep backward for fast flight.

yaw
The angle of a plane when seen from above (or below) – that is, whether it is flying straight ahead, or turning to the left or right. Yaw is controlled by the rudder.

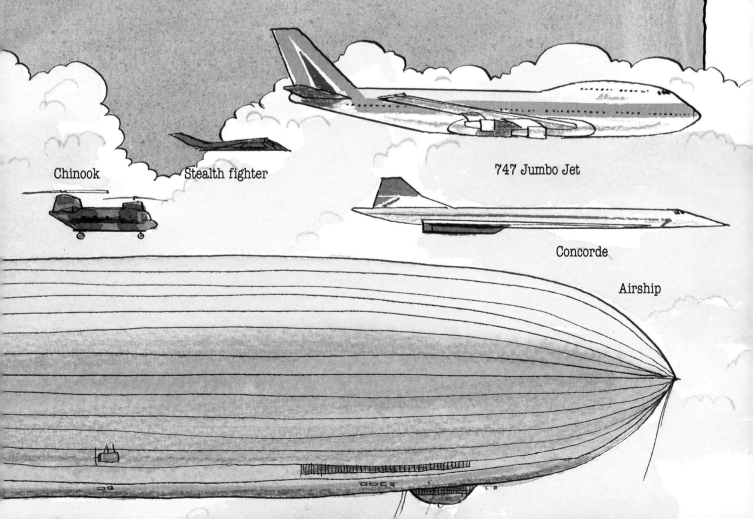

Chinook

Stealth fighter

747 Jumbo Jet

Concorde

Airship

INDEX

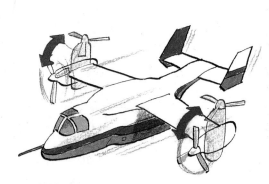